THE FF
OF TH

GW00385616

John Murray

THE BANNER OF TRUTH TRUST

THE BANNER OF TRUTH TRUST
3 Murrayfield Road, Edinburgh EH12 6EL, UK
P.O. Box 621, Carlisle, PA 17013, USA

✻

ISBN 0 85151 817 6

✻

Typeset in 11/13 pt Sabon MT
Printed in Great Britain by
Howie & Seath,
Edinburgh

The Free Offer
of the Gospel

It would appear that the real point in dispute in connection with the free offer of the gospel is whether it can properly be said that God *desires* the salvation of all men. The Committee elected by the Twelfth General Assembly in its report to the Thirteenth General Assembly [of the Orthodox Presbyterian Church] said, 'God not only delights in the penitent but is also moved by the riches of his goodness and mercy to desire the repentance and salvation of the impenitent and reprobate' (*Minutes*, p. 67). It should have been apparent that the aforesaid Committee, in predicating such 'desire' of God, was not dealing with the decretive will of God; it was dealing with the free offer of the gospel to all without distinction and that surely respects, not the decretive or secret will of God, but the revealed will. There is no ground for the supposition that the expression was intended to refer to God's decretive will.

It must be admitted that if the expression were intended to apply to the decretive will of God then there would be, at least, implicit contradiction. For to say that God desires the salvation of the reprobate and also that God wills the damnation of the reprobate and apply the former to the same thing as the latter, namely, the decretive will would be contradiction; it would amount to averring of the same thing, viewed from the same aspect, that God wills and God does not will.

The question then is: what is implicit in, or lies back of, the full and free offer of the gospel to all without distinction? The word 'desire' has come to be used in the debate, not because it is *necessarily* the most accurate or felicitous word but because it serves to set forth quite sharply a certain implication of the full and free offer of the gospel to all. This implication is that in the free offer there is expressed not simply the bare preceptive will of God but the disposition of loving kindness on the part of God pointing to the salvation to be gained through compliance with the overtures of gospel grace. In other words the gospel is not simply an offer or invitation, but also implies that God delights that those to whom the offer comes would enjoy what is offered in all its fullness. And the word 'desire' has been used in order to express the thought epitomized in Ezekiel 33:11, which is to the effect that God has pleasure that the wicked turn from his evil way and live. It might as well have been said, 'It pleases God that the wicked repent and be saved.'

Again, the expression 'God desires', in the formula that crystallizes the crux of the question, is intended to notify not at all the 'seeming' attitude of God but a real attitude, a real disposition of lovingkindness inherent in the free offer to all; in other words, a pleasure or delight in God, contemplating the blessed result to be achieved by compliance with the overture proffered and the invitation given.

Still further, it is necessary to point out that such 'desire' on the part of God for the salvation of all must never be conceived of as desire to such an end apart from the means to that end. It is not desire of their salvation irrespective of repentance and faith. Such would be inconceivable. For it would mean, as Calvin says, 'to renounce the difference between good and evil.' If it is proper to say that God desires the salvation of the reprobate, then he desires such by their repentance And so it amounts to the same thing to say, 'God desires their salvation', as to say, 'He desires their repentance'. This is the same as saying that he desires them to comply with the indispensable conditions of salvation. It would be impossible to say the one without implying the other.

SCRIPTURAL BASIS

The Committee would now respectfully submit some exegetical material bearing upon this question and with a view to the resolution of it.

Matthew 5:44–48.

This passage does not indeed deal with the overtures of grace in the gospel. But it does tell us something regarding God's benevolence that has bearing upon all manifestations of divine grace. The particular aspect of God's grace reflected upon here is the common gifts of providence, the making of the sun to rise upon evil and good and the sending of rain upon just and unjust. There can be no question but all without distinction, reprobate as well as elect, are the beneficiaries of this favour, and it is that fact that is distinctly stated in verse 45.

The significant feature of this text is that this bestowal of favour by God on all alike is adduced as the reason why the disciples are to love their enemies and do them good. There is, of course, a question as to the proper text of verse 44. If we follow the Aleph-B text and omit the clauses, 'Bless them who curse you, do good to them who hate you', as well as the verb 'despitefully use', the sense is not affected. And besides, these clauses, though they may not belong to the genuine text of Matthew, appear in Luke 6:27,28 in practically the same form. Hence the teaching of our Lord undoubtedly was that the disciples were to love their enemies, do good to those who hated them, bless those who cursed them, and pray for those who despitefully used them and persecuted them. And the reason provided is that God himself bestows his favours upon his enemies. The particular reason mentioned why the disciples are to be guided and animated by the divine example is that they, the disciples, are sons of the Father. The obligation and urge to the love of their enemies and the bestowal of good upon them are here grounded in the filial relation that they sustain to God. Since they are sons of God they must be like their heavenly Father. There can be no doubt but that the main point is the necessity of imitating the divine example and this necessity is peculiarly enforced by the consideration of the filial relation they sustain to God as *their* heavenly Father.

It is just here, however, that it becomes necessary to note the implications of the similarity established and enforced as the reason for such attitude and conduct with reference to their enemies. The disciples are to love their enemies in order that they may be the sons of their Father; they must imitate their Father. Clearly implied is the thought that God, the Father, loves his enemies and that it is because he loves his enemies that he makes his sun rise upon them and sends them rain. This is just saying that the kindness bestowed in sunshine and rain is the expression of divine love, that back of the bestowal there is an attitude on the part of God, called love, which constrains him to bestow these tokens of his lovingkindness. This informs us that the gifts bestowed by God are not simply gifts which have the effect of good and blessing to those who are the recipients but that they are also a manifestation or expression of lovingkindness and goodness in the heart or will of God with reference to those who are the recipients. The enjoyment on the part of the recipients has its ground as well as its source in this lovingkindness of which the gifts enjoyed are the expression. In other words these are gifts and are enjoyed because there is in a true and high sense benevolence in the heart of God.

These conclusions are reinforced by verse 48. There can be no question regarding the immediate relevance of verse 48 to the exhortation of verses 44–47, even though it may have a more comprehensive reference. And verse 48 means that what has been adduced by way of divine example in the preceding verses is set forth as epitomizing the divine perfection and as providing the great exemplar by which the believer's attitude and conduct are to be governed and the goal to which thought and life are to be oriented. The love and beneficence of God to the evil and unjust epitomize the norm of human perfection. It is obvious that this love and beneficence on the part of God are regarded by our Lord himself as not something incidental in God but as that which constitutes an element in the sum of divine perfection. This is made very specific in the parallel passage in Luke 6:35,36 where we read, 'And ye shall be sons of the Most High, because he is kind towards the unthankful and evil. Ye shall be merciful, as your Father is merciful.' This word translated 'merciful' is redolent of the pity and compassion in the heart of God that overflow in the bestowments of kindness.

The sum of this study of these passages in Matthew and Luke is simply this, that presupposed in God's gifts bestowed upon the ungodly there is in God a disposition of love, kindness, mercifulness, and that the actual gifts and the blessing accruing therefrom for the ungodly must not be abstracted from the lovingkindness of which they are the expression. And, of course, we must not think of this lovingkindness as conditioned upon a penitent attitude in the recipients. The lovingkindness rather is exercised towards them in their ungodly state and is expressed in the favours they enjoy. What bearing this may have upon the grace of God manifested in the free offer of the gospel to all without distinction remains to be seen. But we are hereby given a disclosure of goodness in the heart of God and of the relation there is between gifts bestowed and the lovingkindness from which they flow. And there is indicated to us something respecting God's love or benevolence that we might not or could not entertain if we concentrated our thought simply on the divine decree of reprobation. Furthermore we must remember that there are many gifts enjoyed by the ungodly who are within the pale of the gospel administration which are not enjoyed by those outside, and we shall have to conclude that in respect of these specific favours, enjoyed by such ungodly persons in distinction from others, the same principle of divine benevolence and lovingkindness must obtain, a lovingkindness, too, which must correspond to the character of the specific gifts enjoyed.

Acts 14:17.

This text does not express as much as those considered already. But it does witness to the same truth that God gave testimony to his own perfection when he did good to those whom he left to walk in their own ways. God did them good, he sent them rain from heaven and fruitful seasons, filling their hearts with food and gladness. We must infer, on the basis of what we found already, that behind this doing of good and bestowal of blessing, as well as behind the gladness of heart which followed, there was the divine goodness and lovingkindness.

Deuteronomy 5:29 (26 in Hebrew); 32:29; Psalm 81:13 ff. (81:14 ff. in Hebrew); Isaiah 48:18.

The purpose of adducing these texts is to note the optative[1] force of that which is expressed. There can be no reasonable question as to the optative force of Deuteronomy 5:29(26). It is introduced by the idiom *mi yitten* which literally means 'who will give?' but is really a strong optative expression meaning, 'Oh that there were!' Consequently the text reads, 'Oh that there were such a heart in them, that they would fear me, and keep all my commandments always, that it might be well with them, and with their children for ever!' It is the Lord who is speaking and we shall have to conclude that here we have the expression of earnest desire or wish or will that the people of Israel were of a heart to fear him and keep all his commandments always. It is appareut from the book of Deuteronomy itself (cf. 31:24–29) and from the whole history of Israel that they did not have a heart to fear God and to keep all his commandments always. Since they did not fulfil that which was optatively expressed in 5:29 (26), we must conclude that God had not decreed that they should have such a heart. If God had decreed it, it would have been so. Here therefore we have an instance of desire

[1] Optative = expressing a wish or a desire.

on the part of God for the fulfilment of that which he had not decreed, in other words, a will on the part of God to that which he had not decretively willed.

In Deuteronomy 32:29 the construction is somewhat different. In our English versions it is translated, 'Oh that they were wise, that they understood this, that they would consider their latter end.' This rendering is distinctly optative and has the same effect as Deuteronomy 5:29 (26), considered above. It must be admitted that this is a perfectly legitimate rendering and interpretation. The conjunction *lu* with which the verse begins has undoubtedly this optative force. It has such force unquestionably in Genesis 17:18; Numbers 14:2; 20:3; 22:29; Joshua 7:7; Isaiah 63:19, and possibly, if not probably, in Genesis 23:13; 30:34. When *lu* has this optative force it means 'Oh that' or 'if only' and expresses strong desire. In view of what we found in Deuteronomy 5:26 there is no reason why the optative force of *lu* should not be adopted here. We may not, however, insist that *lu* must have optative force here because *lu* is also used with conditional force, as in Judges 8:19; 13:23; 2 Samuel 18:12 and elsewhere. If *lu* is understood conditionally, Deuteronomy 32:29 would be rendered as follows: 'If they were wise, they would understand this, they would consider their latter end.' This, however, is not the most natural rendering. The optative interpretation is smoother and more meaningful in the context. If this more natural construction is followed it shows the same thing as we found in Deuteronomy 5:26, that earnest desire is expressed for what is contrary to fact (cf. v. 28).

In Psalm 81:14 it may readily be detected that the conditional force of the conjunction *lu* cannot reasonably be adopted. The thought is rather distinctly optative, 'Oh that my people were hearkening unto me, that Israel would walk in my ways.'

Isaiah 48:18 could readily be rendered conditionally thus: 'If thou hadst hearkened to my commandments, thy peace had been as a river and thy righteousness as the waves of the sea.' It can also be rendered optatively as in our English versions.

It should be noted that even when the conjunction *lu* is given very distinct conditional force, the optative idea is sometimes rather noticeably in the background. This would very likely be the case in Isaiah 48:18 even if the optative rendering gives way to the conditional. The desirableness of that which is expressed in the condition and its corresponding consequence cannot be suppressed. This can be expressed in our English idiom very well when we render, If only thou hadst hearkened to my commandments, then had thy peace been as a river', etc. Both the conditional and optative appear here, and there is much to be said in favour of the conclusion that, whether we render Isaiah 48:18 optatively or conditionally, the optative notion still persists, in the former case, of course. directly and in the latter case indirectly.

Should we make full allowance for doubts as to the exact force of the construction in the case of Deuteronomy 32:29 and Isaiah 48:18, there can be no room for question but that the Lord represents himself in some of these passages as earnestly desiring the fulfilment of something which he had not in the exercise of his sovereign will actually decreed to come to pass. This bears very directly upon the point at issue.

Matthew 23:37; Luke 13:34.

In this passage there should be no dispute that the will of Christ in the direction of a certain benign result is set in contrast with the will of those who are contemplated as the subjects of such blessing. These two stand in opposition to each other – I have willed (or wished), ye have not willed (or wished). Not only so. The will of Christ to a certain end is opposed to that which actually occurred. Jesus says he often wished the occurrence of something which did not come to pass and therefore willed (or wished) the occurrence of that which God had not secretly or decretively willed.

That which Jesus wished is stated to be the gathering together of the children of Jerusalem, as a hen gathers together her chickens under her wings. This surely means the gathering together of the people of Jerusalem under his saving and protecting grace. So we have the most emphatic declaration on the part of Christ of his having yearned for the conversion and salvation of the people of Jerusalem.

It might be said that Jesus is here giving expression simply to his human desire and that this would not indicate, therefore, the desire or will of God. In other words, it might be said that we are not justified in transferring this expression of his human desire to the *divine* desire or will, either in respect of Jesus' own divine consciousness or the divine consciousness of the other persons of the Godhead.

Christ was indeed truly human and his human mind and will operated within the limitations inseparable from human nature. His human nature was not omniscient and could not in the nature of the case be cognisant of the whole decretive will of God. In his human nature he wrought within limits that could not apply to the specifically divine knowledge, desire and will. Hence it might be argued that on this occasion he gave expression to the yearnings of his truly human will and therefore to a will that could not be aware of the whole secret purpose of God. Furthermore, it might be said that Jesus was speaking of what he willed in the past before he was aware, in his human consciousness, of the judgment that was to befall Jerusalem, stated in verses 38, 39. A great deal more might be said along this line that would lend plausibility to such an interpretation.

We are not able to regard such an interpretation of our Lord's statement as tenable. It is true our Lord was human. It is true he spoke as human. And it is true he spoke these words or gave utterance to this lament through the medium of his human nature. The will he spoke of on this occasion was certainly one that engaged the total exercise of his human desire and will. But there is much more that needs to be considered if we are properly to assess the significance of this incident and of Jesus' utterance. Jesus is speaking here in his capacity as the Messiah and Saviour. He is speaking therefore as the God-man. He is speaking of the will on his part as the Messiah and Saviour to embrace the people of Jerusalem in the arms of his saving grace and covenant love.

The majesty that belongs to his person in this unique capacity shines through the whole episode and it is quite improper to abstract the divine aspect of his person from the capacity in which he gives utterance to this will and from the prerogative in virtue of which he could give expression to the utterance.

What needs to be appreciated is that the embrace of which Jesus here speaks is that which he exercises in that unique office and prerogative that belong to him as the God-man Messiah and Saviour. In view of the transcendent, divine function which he says he wished to perform, it would be illegitimate for us to say that here we have simply an example of his human desire or will. It is surely, therefore, a revelation to us of the divine will as well as of the human.

Our Lord in the exercise of his most specific and unique function as the God-man gives expression to a yearning will on his part that responsiveness on the part of the people of Jerusalem would have provided the necessary condition for the bestowal of his saving and protecting love, a responsiveness, nevertheless, which it was not the decretive will of God to create in their hearts.

In this connection we must not fail to keep in mind the principle borne out by Jesus' own repeated declarations, especially as recorded in the Gospel of John, namely, the perfect harmony and coalescence of will on the part of the Father and of the Son (cf. John 12:49, 50; 14:10, 24; 17:8) To aver that Jesus in the expressed will of Matthew 23:37 is not disclosing the *divine* will but simply his own human will would tend towards very grave prejudice to this principle. And, viewing the matter from the standpoint of revelation, how would it affect our conception of Jesus as the supreme revelation of the Father if in this case we were not to regard his words as a transcript of the Father's will as well as of his own? We can readily see the difficulties that face us if we do not grant the truly *revelatory* significance of our Lord's statement.

In this lament over Jerusalem, furthermore, there is surely disclosed to us something of the will of our Lord as the Son of God and divine Son of man that lies back of, and is expressed in, such an invitation as Matthew 11:28. Here we have declared, if we may use the thought of Matthew 23:37, his will to embrace the labouring and heavy laden in the arms of his saving and loving protection. And it is an invitation to all such to take advantage of that will of his. The fulness and freeness of the invitation need not now be argued. Its character as such is patent. It is important, however, to note that the basis and background of this invitation are supplied by the uniqueness of the relation that he sustains to the Father as the Son, the transcendent commission that is given to him as the Son, and the sovereignty, coordinate with that of the Father, which he exercises because of that unique relationship and in that unique capacity. We should not fail to perceive the interrelations of these two passages (Matthew 23:37; 11:28) and to recognize that the former is redolent of his divine prerogative and revelatory of his divine will. Verses 38 and 39 confirm the high prerogative in terms of which he is speaking, for there he pronounces the divine judgment. And in this connection we cannot forget John 5:26, 27, 'For as the Father hath life in himself, even so hath he given to the Son to have life in himself. And he hath given to him authority to execute judgment, because he is the Son of man.'

Ezekiel 18:23, 32; 33:11.

It does not appear to us in the least justifiable to limit the reference of these passages to any one class of wicked persons. Suffice it now to mention one or two considerations in support of this conclusion. In Ezekiel 33:4–9 the wicked who actually die in their iniquity are contemplated. It is without warrant to exclude such wicked persons from the scope of the wicked spoken of in verse 11. While it is true that a new paragraph may be regarded as introduced at verse 10, yet the new thought of verse 10 is simply the despairing argument or objection on the part of the house of Israel and does not have the effect of qualifying the denotation or connotation of the wicked mentioned in verse 11, a denotation and a connotation determined by the preceding verses. Again, the emphatic negative of the first part of verse 11 – 'I have no pleasure in the death of the wicked' – admits of no limitation or qualification; it applies to the wicked who actually die in their iniquity. Why then should there be the least disposition to limit those spoken of in the text to any class of wicked persons?

In Ezekiel 18:23 the construction is not without significance. This verse is introduced by the interrogative and then we have the emphatic construction of duplication well known in Hebrew. It might be rendered, 'Taking pleasure in, do I take pleasure in?' The question implies, of course, an emphatic negative. It should also be noted that the verb in this case takes a direct object, namely 'the death of the wicked' (*moth rasha*, without any article). In this case we do not have the preposition *be* as in Ezekiel 33:11.[1] It should be noted that the verb *chapez* with such a construction can very properly be rendered by our English word, 'desire', as frequently elsewhere in the Old Testament. Consequently this verse may well be rendered, 'Do I at all desire the death of the wicked?' The force of this is obviously the emphatic negative, 'I do not by any means desire the death of the wicked', or, to be very literal, 'I do not by any means desire death of a wicked person.'

The interrogative construction is continued in the latter part of the verse. Here. however, it is negative in form, implying an affirmative answer to the question, just as in the former part the affirmative form implied a negative answer. It reads, 'Is it not rather in his turning from his way (the Massoretes read 'his ways') and live.' The clear import is an emphatic asseveration to the effect that the Lord Jehovah delights rather in the turning of the wicked from his evil way that he may live.

---

[1] Kittel says that 20 manuscripts read *bemoth* as in verse 32. If this reading is correct, then, of course, what is said respecting the omission of the preposition *be* does not hold.

The adversative form of the sentence may well be rendered thus: 'Do I at all desire the death of the wicked, saith the Lord Jehovah, and not rather that he turn from his way and live?'

The sum of the matter may be stated in the following propositions. It is absolutely and universally true that God does not delight in or desire the death of a wicked person. It is likewise absolutely and universally true that he delights in the repentance and life of that wicked person. It would surely be quite unwarranted to appy the latter proposition less universally or more restrictively than the former. The adversative construction and the emphatic form by which the protestation is introduced are surely not compatible with any other conclusion. And if we carry over the perfectly proper rendering of the first clause, the thought can be expressed thus, 'God does not desire the death of the wicked but rather their repentance and life.'

In Ezekiel 33:11 the construction is somewhat different. The statement is introduced by the oath, 'As I live, saith the Lord Jehovah'. Then we have the construction with the Hebrew *im*, which has the force of an emphatic negative and must be rendered, I have no delight (or pleasure) in the death of the wicked' (*bemoth harasha;* in this case the article is used). It should be noted that the preposition *be* is used in this case, as also in the second part of 18:23 as observed below.[1] This is a very frequent construction in Hebrew with reference to delight in persons or things. Interesting examples are 2 Samuel 24:3; Esther 6:6, 7, 9, 11;

[1] The only instances we have been able to find in the Old Testament of *chapez be*, followed by the infinitive construct, are Ezekiel 18:23b and 33:11b; *chapez* without the preposition *be* is found in other cases, cf. Isaiah 53:10.

Psalm 147:10; Proverbs 18:2; Isaiah 65:12; Malachi 2:17. On certain occasions the Hebrew word could well be translated 'desire' in English and the word that follows the preposition taken as the direct object (e.g., 2 Samuel 24:3).

It has been argued that the preposition *be* in Ezekiel 33:11b has the force of 'when', so that the verse would read, 'As I live, saith the Lord Jehovah, I have no pleasure in the death of the wicked but *when* the wicked turns from his way and lives.' And so it has been claimed that all that is said in this verse is that God is pleased *when* the wicked turns and that it cannot be made to support the proposition that God is pleased *that* the wicked should repent, whether they repent or not. On this view it would be maintained that this verse says nothing more than that God is pleased when a wicked man repents, but says nothing respecting the pleasure of God in reference to the repentance of those who do not actually repent.

In dealing with this question a few things need to be said.

i. A study of the instances where this construction of the verb *chaphez* with the preposition *be* occurs would not suggest this interpretation of the force of the preposition *be*. The usage rather indicates that the preposition points to that upon which pleasure is placed, that to which desire gravitates, that in which delight is taken. That object of pleasure, desire, delight may he conceived of as existing, or as something not actually existent, or as something desirable, that is to say, desired to be. When the object is contemplated as desirable, but not actually realized, the thought of *chaphez* does not at all appear to be simply that delight or pleasure will be derived from the object when it is realized or possessed. That thought is, of course, implied. But there is much more. There is the delight or pleasure or desire that it should come to be, even if

[18]

the actual occurrence should never take place. Consequently it appears that the notion that Ezekiel 33:11b simply says that God is pleased *when* a wicked man repents robs the concept expressed by *chaphez be* of some of its most characteristic and necessary meaning. It is not in any way denied that this kind of delight is embraced in the expression. But to limit the concept to this notion is without warrant and is not borne out by the usage.

ii. The adversative construction of the verse would not by any means suggest the interpretation that verse 11b says simply that God is pleased *when* a man repents. In the same clause it is denied that God has pleasure in the death of the wicked. In accordance with 18:23 this means that it is true absolutely and universally that God does not delight in the death of the wicked. This does not mean simply that God does not delight in the death of the wicked *when* he dies. The denial is much more embracive. In like manner, it would be unnatural for us to suppose that the affirmation of that in which God does take delight is simply the turning of the wicked from his way *when* it occurs. This is just saying that it is natural to give to the preposition *be* in the second clause the same force as it has in the first. Rendered literally then the two clauses would read, 'I do not have pleasure in the death of the wicked but rather in his turning from his way and that he live.' Paraphrased the thought would be, 'It is not pleasing to me that the wicked die but that the wicked turn from his way and live.' And the same kind of absoluteness and universality denied in the one case must be regarded as affirmed in the other.

iii. Confirmation of this interpretation may be derived from the concluding clauses of verse 11, 'Turn ye, turn ye from your evil ways, and why will ye die, O house of Israel?' The thought of the last clause is that there is no reason why they should die. There is no reason because of the grace so emphatically declared in the earlier part of the verse and, by implication, so fully and freely proferred. There will not be any dispute regarding the universality of the exhortation and command in the clause, 'Turn ye, turn ye from your evil ways.' This is a command that applies to all men without any discrimination or exception. It expresses therefore the will of God to repentance. He wills that all should repent. Nothing less than that is expressed in the universal command. To state the matter more fully, he wills that all should repent and live or be saved. When this is related to the last clause, 'Why will ye die?', it means that the reason why no one need die, why there is no reason why any should die, is, that God does not will that any should die. He wills rather that they repent and live.

This declaration of the will of God to the repentance and life of all, so clearly implied in the two concluding clauses, rests, however, upon the declarations of the two preceding clauses, the clauses with which we are now more particularly concerned. We should conclude, therefore, that the will to universal repentance and life, so unmistakably expressed in the concluding clauses, is also declared or, at least, implied in the words, 'I have no pleasure in the death of the wicked but that the wicked turn from his way and live.' This is just saying that the import of the hortatory and interrogative clauses at the end requires or presupposes a will of God to repentance and life, a will to which the bare notion that God is pleased *when* men repent is not by any means equal. The only adequate way of expressing the will implied in the exhortation is the will that all should repent and it is surely that truth that is declared in the oath-supported statement, 'I have no pleasure in the death of the wicked, but that the wicked turn from his way and live.'

It is not to be forgotten that when it is said that God absolutely and universally takes no pleasure in the death of the wicked, we are not here speaking of God's decretive will. In terms of his decretive will it must be said that God absolutely decrees the eternal death of some wicked and, in that sense, is absolutely pleased so to decree. But in the text it is the will of God's benevolence (*voluntas euarestias*) that is stated, not the will of God's decree (*voluntas eudokias*). It is, in our judgment, quite unjustifiable to think that in this passage there is any reflection upon the decretive will of God in the word *chaphez*. And neither is there evidence to show that in the word *chaphez* there is here any comparative notion to the effect that God takes greater pleasure in saving men than he does in damning them.

It is indeed true that in a few passages in the Old Testament the word *chaphez* is used with reference to the decretive will of God (cf. Psalm 115:3; 135:6; the substantive *chephez*, also, in Isaiah 44:28; 46:10; 48:14). But in this passage everything points to the conclusion that the good pleasure or delight of God spoken of is viewed entirely from the aspect of benevolent lovingkindness. And it is in terms of that aspect of the divine will that the words 'absolutely' and 'universally' have been used above.

Isaiah 45:22

There can be no question but the salvation mentioned in this text is salvation in the highest sense. It cannot be weakened to mean temporary or temporal security. The salvation must be of the same character as that referred to in verse 17 and implied in the title appropriated by God himself in verse 21. The text is also an invitation and command to all to turn to God and to be saved. The universalism of this command should be apparent from the expression 'all the ends of the earth'. This is a characteristic Old Testament phrase to designate all nations and peoples. The universal scope is, however, confirmed by the context. There are several intimations of this. In the preceding context the Lord asserts his Creatorhood (verses 12, 18). This appeal to his Creatorhood has the effect of bringing to the forefront a relationship which he sustains to all men alike. Likewise the Lord protests that he is the only God, that there is none else besides him (verse 14, 18, 21). The emphasis on this becomes more specific in the repeated assertion that he alone is the Saviour (verses 15, 20, 21). Furthermore, that all men are contemplated is borne out by verse 23, that unto him every knee shall bow, every tongue shall swear. Finally, this note is implied in the scorn that is poured out upon the heathen in verse 20 – 'They have not knowledge that carry the wood of their graven image, and pray unto a god that cannot save.' All these considerations bear directly upon the universal reference of the appeal in verse 22. It is because God alone is God and because he alone can save that the exhortation is extended to all, 'Turn ye to me and be ye saved.' We could not place any kind of limitation upon the exhortation without interfering with the universality of the prerogatives claimed by God himself in the context. It is necessary to stress this because it might be thought that the universalism of the command in verse 22 is not distributive universalism but simply ethnical universalism, all nations without distinction but not all people without exception. The considerations of the context would show that there is no exception to the command any more than there is to the sole Creatorhood, sole Godhood and sole Saviourhood of the God who extends the appeal.

This text expresses then the will of God in the matter of the call, invitation, appeal, and command of the gospel, namely, the will that all should turn to him and be saved. What God wills in this sense he certainly is pleased to will. If it is his pleasure to will that all repent and be saved, it is surely his pleasure that all repent and be saved. Obviously, however, it is not his decretive will that all repent and be saved. While, on the one hand, he has not decretively willed that all be saved, yet he declares unequivocally that it is his will and, impliedly, his pleasure that all turn and be saved. We are again faced with the mystery and adorable richness of the divine will. It might seem to us that the one rules out the other. But it is not so. There is a multiformity to the divine will that is consonant with the fulness and richness of his divine character, and it is no wonder that we are constrained to bow in humble yet exultant amazement before his ineffable greatness and unsearchable judgments. To deny the reality of the divine pleasure directed to the repentance and salvation of all is to fail to accept the witness borne by such a text as this to the manifoldness of God's will and the riches of his grace.

2 Peter 3:9

In view of what we have found already there is no reason in *the analogy of Scripture* why we should not regard this passage as teaching that God in the exercise of his benevolent longsuffering and lovingkindness wills that none should perish, but that all should come to repentance. An *a priori* assumption that this text cannot teach that God wills the repentance and salvation of all is a gravely unsound assumption, for it is not an assumption derived from the analogy of Scripture. In approaching this text there should be no such prejudice. What this text does actually teach will have to be determined, however, by grammatico-historical exegesis of the text and context.

The choice of the verb 'is longsuffering' (*makrothumei*) will be considered first. In Luke 18:7, the only other instance in the New Testament where it refers to the action of God, it probably relates to the elect. But in that case it is employed in the somewhat distinctive sense of 'delay' in avenging them. The longsuffering (*makrothumia*) of God, is spoken of several times, and its usage is illuminating. Romans 9:22 presents a clear instance where it has in view an attitude of God towards the reprobate; he 'endured with much longsuffering vessels of wrath'. In Romans 2:4, it is associated with the goodness and forbearance of God, and subsumed under his goodness, as that which is despised by the impenitent who treasures up for himself wrath in the day of wrath, who does not know that the goodness of God 'leadeth him to repentance (*eis metanoian se agei*). The choice of the verb *agein* is to be noted. Since the impenitent are in view, it cannot refer to efficacious grace. Nevertheless, it is a strong verb, as its use in Romans 8:14 shows: 'As many as are led by the Spirit of God, these are the sons of God' (cf. Galatians 5:18). It must be understood as a constraining influence flowing from the goodness of God which is calculated to bring men to repentance. The construction in Romans 2:4 is remarkably similar to that in 2 Peter 3:9.

On the background of these passages, the usage by Peter may be considered to advantage. In the last days, Peter says, mockers will mock because the *parousia* has not come. The day of judgment will nevertheless come. The apparent delay in its coming some count slackness. What is counted as slackness by some should, however, really be recognized as longsuffering (2 Peter 3:3–9). The longsuffering should not be counted as slackness, but as salvation (verse 15). The long-suffering is, then, a positive favour of God towards sinners which is directed to their salvation.

Up to this point, accordingly, the thought is similar to that of Romans 2:4. Men may despise God's goodness, forbearance and longsuffering towards them, not knowing that that goodness has in view their turning from their sins to God. Men may count the longsuffering as slackness on God's part, when actually they ought to account it as designed to extend salvation to them.

But this tentative judgment on the basis of the use of *makrothumia* must be related to the rest of verse 9. This aspect of the question is considerably complicated by the divergence in the textual tradition at this point. The situation is reflected in part in the divergence between Authorized Version and American Revised Version: 'to us-ward' and 'to you-ward'. But there is a further complication due to the fact that there is significant testimony for the preposition *dia,* resulting in the possibilities: 'on your account' or 'on our account'. The reading *dia* has come to be preferred by Mayor, Moffatt, Greijdanus, and the Revised Standard Version margin. The difference between 'you' and 'us' or 'your' and 'our' is not especially significant, since in either case the readers of the Epistle would be primarily in view. The actual line-up of authorities does not, however, leave solid external support for the combination 'on our account', though Mayor supports it. The reading 'to us-ward' is clearly the weakest reading, judged by external evidence; and it is not commended particularly by other considerations. Hence the choice falls between 'to you-ward' and 'on your account'. While perhaps it is not possible to decide finally between these two readings, we may judge that the reading 'on your account' has a very strong claim. The external evidence for it appears to be at least as strong as for the other competing reading, and transcriptionally it may be preferred as being somewhat more unusual and difficult.

The question now arises as to the specific reference of 'you', whether with the preposition *dia* or *eis*. Does the use of this pronoun indicate that reprobate men are out of consideration here? So it has been argued. However, if the reprobate are out of consideration here, the 'true believers' would have to be identified with the elect, and the longsuffering of God would have to be understood as the special, saving grace of God manifested to the elect alone. We do not believe that the restriction of the reference to the elect is well-established. The Epistle does not make this restriction. Moreover, since on this view, the believers addressed here are characterized as 'living lax Christian lives', are viewed as requiring repentance, and even as about to 'perish' unless they repent, it cannot be argued plausibly that the apostle would not have allowed for the presence of some reprobate among the members of his audience. Even if the 'you' is restricted to professing Christians, one cannot exclude the possibility that reprobate men were also in view.

The 'you' of this passage can hardly be restricted to the elect. Can it even be restricted to 'believers'? Can it be restricted to believers who urgently stand in need of repent-ance? The determination of this question is bound up with the evaluation of the subordinate clauses. It may be acknowledged that the decision made with regard to 'you' will bear upon the meaning of the language that follows. But the reverse is also true. The language of the clauses may be such as to reflect decisively upon the persons referred to in connection with the manifestations of longsuffering. Does not, as a matter of fact, the language, 'not wishing that any should perish, but that all should come to repentance', set before us a basic antithesis between the *death* or destruction that awaits impenitent sinners and, by implication, the *life* eternal which men may enter upon through repentance? God does not wish that any men should perish. His wish is rather that all should enter upon life eternal by coming to repentance. The language in this part of the verse is so absolute that it is highly unnatural to envisage Peter as meaning merely that God does not wish that any believers should perish, but rather wishes that all believers who live laxly should repent of their sins. If they are believers, they have already come to repentance, entered upon life, and escaped destruction, even though the struggle against sin and turning from it must continue. The language of the clauses, then, most naturally refers to mankind as a whole as men are faced with the issues of death or life before the day of judgment comes. It does not view men either as elect or as reprobate, and so allows that both elect and reprobate make up the totality in view.

The most satisfactory view of 2 Peter 3:9 is:

i. Peter teaches that the delay of the coming of judgment should be acknowledged as a manifestation of the longsuffering or patience of God with sinners.

ii. Peter says that God is longsuffering *on your account*. It is not because of any slackness in God himself, but because of the consideration of the well-being of men. The pronoun 'you' cannot be restricted to the elect. It would certainly include the members of the Christian community as possible benefactors of the longsuffering of God, but in view of considerations adduced above may not fairly be restricted to believers.

iii. If the reading 'to you-ward' is adopted, the thrust of the passage is not essentially altered. The delay is not due to slackness in God, but is to be regarded as an expression of longsuffering towards men, including very specifically those addressed in the Epistle.

iv. The reason or ground for the longsuffering of God until the day of judgment is given in what is said concerning his 'willing'. He is longsuffering in that, or because, he does not wish that any men should perish, but rather because he wills or wishes that all should come to repentance. Repentance is the condition of life; without repentance men must perish. But the will of God that men be saved expressed here is not conditional. It is not: I will your salvation if you repent; but: I will that you repent and thus be saved. The two clauses then go far beyond defining the longsuffering of God, for they intimate what is back of his longsuffering. This favour is grounded in God himself; it is an expression of his will with regard to sinners, his will being nothing short of their salvation

The argument that the longsuffering of God that delays judgment could not concern the reprobate, 'for they will never repent', is to be met exactly as Calvin met similar arguments. Following his exegesis of 2 Peter 3:9, Calvin says: 'But it may be asked, If God wishes none to perish, why is it that so many perish? To this my answer is, that no mention is here made of the hidden purpose of God, according to which the reprobate are doomed to their own ruin, but only of his will as made known to us in the gospel. For God there stretches out his hand without a difference to all, but lays hold only of those, to lead them unto himself, whom he has chosen before the foundation of the world.'

CONCLUSIONS

i. We have found that the grace of God bestowed in his ordinary providence expresses the love of God, and that this love of God is the source of the gifts bestowed upon and enjoyed by the ungodly as well as the godly. We should expect that herein is disclosed to us a principle that applies to all manifestations of divine grace, namely, that the grace bestowed expresses the lovingkindness in the heart of God and that the gifts bestowed are in their respective variety tokens of a correspondent richness or manifoldness in the divine lovingkindness of which they are the expression.

ii. We have found that God himself expresses an ardent desire for the fulfilment of certain things which he has not decreed in his inscrutable counsel to come to pass. This means that there is a will to the realization of what he has not decretively willed, a pleasure towards that which he has not been pleased to decree. This is indeed mysterious, and why he has not brought to pass, in the exercise of his omnipotent power and grace, what is his ardent pleasure lies hid in the sovereign counsel of his will. We should not entertain, however, any prejudice against the notion that God desires or has pleasure in the accomplishment of what he does not decretively will.

iii. Our Lord himself in the exercise of his messianic prerogative provides us with an example of the foregoing as it applies to the matter of salvation. He says expressly that he willed the bestowal of his saving and protecting grace upon those whom neither the Father nor he decreed thus to save and protect.

iv. We found that God reveals himself as not taking pleasure in or desiring the death of those who die but rather as taking pleasure in or desiring the repentance and life of the wicked. This will of God to repentance and salvation is universalized and reveals to us, therefore, that there is in God a benevolent lovingkindness towards the repentance and salvation of even those whom he has not decreed to save. This pleasure, will, desire is expressed in the universal call to repentance.

v. We must conclude, therefore, that our provisional inference on the basis of Matthew 5:44–48 is borne out by the other passages. The full and free offer of the gospel is a grace bestowed upon all. Such grace is necessarily a manifestation of love or lovingkindness in the heart of God. And this lovingkindness is revealed to be of a character or kind that is correspondent with the grace bestowed. The grace offered is nothing less than salvation in its richness and fulness. The love or lovingkindness that lies back of that offer is not anything less; it is the will to that salvation. In other words, it is Christ in all the glory of his person and in all the perfection of his finished work whom God offers in the gospel. The loving and benevolent will that is the source of that offer and that grounds its veracity and reality is the will to the possession of Christ and the enjoyment of the salvation that resides in him.

Also by John Murray:

REDEMPTION: ACCOMPLISHED
AND APPLIED

'This volume deals with themes which lie at the very heart
of the Christian faith. Every chapter is worth reading and
re-reading. It should have a place on the shelves of every
student and minister of the Word.'

– W. J. Grier

ISBN 0 85151 119 8
192 pp. Paperback

COLLECTED WRITINGS
OF JOHN MURRAY

These four volumes illustrate John Murray's firmly-held
conviction that theology should be 'shot through with
ardent devotion'. They bring together the most important of
his shorter writings, his major articles and lectures on system-
atic theology, his principal sermons and reviews, and his longer
articles for the *Westminster Theological Review,* together with
a biographical account by Iain H. Murray.

Set of Four Volumes
ISBN 0 85151 396 4
each approximately 400 pp,
clothbound